SAMURAI

by Christine Heppermann

Content Consultant
Stephen Turnbull
Visiting Professor of Japanese Studies
Akita International University, Japan

CORE
LIBRARY

Published by ABDO Publishing Company, PO Box 398166, Minneapolis, MN 55439. Copyright © 2013 by Abdo Consulting Group, Inc. International copyrights reserved in all countries. No part of this book may be reproduced in any form without written permission from the publisher. The Core Library™ is a trademark and logo of ABDO Publishing Company.

Printed in the United States of America, North Mankato, Minnesota
112012
012013

♻ THIS BOOK CONTAINS AT LEAST 10% RECYCLED MATERIALS.

Editor: Lauren Coss
Series Designer: Becky Daum

Cataloging-in-Publication Data
Heppermann, Christine.
 Samurai / Christine Heppermann.
   p. cm. -- (Great warriors)
Includes bibliographical references and index.
ISBN 978-1-61783-727-2
1. Samurai--Juvenile literature.   1. Title.
952.03--dc22

                                    2012946371

Photo Credits: Private Collection/Look and Learn/The Bridgeman Art Library, cover, 1; MIXA/Getty Images, 4; Bernard Allum/iStockphoto, 7, 45; Japanese School (20th century)/Private Collection/Peter Newark Pictures/The Bridgeman Art Library, 9; Look and Learn/The Bridgeman Art Library, 11; iStockphoto/Thinkstock, 12, 24; North Wind/North Wind Picture Archives, 14; Dorling Kindersley RF/Thinkstock, 17, 29; Antonio Abrignani/Shutterstock Images, 19; DeAgostini/Getty Images, 20; Red Line Editorial, 22; Archives Charmet/The Bridgeman Art Library, 27; Maxim Tupikov/Shutterstock Images, 32; Bettmann/Corbis/AP Images, 35; Danita Delimont/Getty Images, 36; V&A Images/Alamy, 38; Shizuo Kambayshi/AP Images, 40

CONTENTS

CHAPTER ONE

LOYALTY ABOVE ALL

It was 1336 CE. The great samurai warrior Kusunoki Masashige was preparing for what he believed would be his final battle. Emperor Go-Daigo, the ruler of Japan, was in danger. Go-Daigo's followers had spent the last five years battling the forces of the shogun. The shogun was a military leader who was supposed to serve the emperor. The shogun governed the rural eastern provinces beyond the

A statue of samurai Kusunoki Masashige still stands in Tokyo, Japan.

capital city of Kyoto. Go-Daigo thought the shogun's government had become too powerful. He vowed to overthrow it.

Kusunoki and the emperor's troops had managed to hold their own against the enemy so far. But the shogun's army was much larger than the emperor's.

Kusunoki was not hopeful about the upcoming battle. Still, as a samurai warrior, Kusunoki was devoted to follow his leader into battle. He would defend Go-Daigo to the death.

Emperor's Orders

Kusunoki was preparing to follow a strategy he felt sure would fail. He had tried to convince Go-Daigo to send his

Emperor Go-Daigo

Go-Daigo became the ninety-sixth emperor of Japan in 1318. But important members of his administration had accused him of plotting to overthrow the shogun's government. He was forced to give up the throne in 1331. Go-Daigo was no longer in power when Kusunoki first pledged his loyalty to the emperor. From 1333 to 1336, Go-Daigo fought to regain his throne and defeat the shogun. This period is known as the Kemmu Restoration.

Samurai were expected to defend their leaders to the death.

army to Mount Hiei. From the higher ground, Go-Daigo's troops could more easily defend against an attack. They could wait for more soldiers to join them.

Go-Daigo had a different plan. He believed heaven supported their cause. It did not matter how large the opposing army was. The gods would protect his troops. Go-Daigo ordered Kusunoki's troops to travel to the southwestern coastal town of Hyogo. At Hyogo they would join with another general's forces.

Seppuku

Seppuku, or suicide, was considered more honorable for a samurai than dying at the hands of an enemy. Samurai believed that the belly held a person's spirit. A deadly belly wound would release the spirit from the body, they believed.

Kusunoki was a samurai. That meant he valued loyalty to his leader more than anything else, even if that loyalty meant certain death. He called his ten-year-old son to his side. He reminded his son of a samurai's duty. Kusunoki told the boy to stay loyal

8

A samurai would rather take his own life with seppuku than be killed or taken prisoner.

to the emperor. Never give up, even if victory seems impossible, he said.

Kusunoki proved his loyalty to his emperor at the Battle of Minato River in 1336. The battle lasted for hours. Kusunoki and his army fought bravely. But the shogun's forces overpowered Go-Daigo's army.

Soon Kusunoki knew for certain that his side could not possibly win. Instead of being killed, he chose to commit *seppuku*, or suicide.

Fighting Smart

This was not Kusunoki's first time fighting for his emperor. Kusunoki took command of Go-Daigo's troops in 1331. He had protected the emperor without fail ever since. He fought bravely in many clashes with the shogun's men. The imperial troops were often greatly outnumbered. But the emperor's soldiers managed to fight off their opponents under the samurai's clever direction.

Kusunoki was smart and brave. In 1331 the shogun's army laid siege to the emperor's Akasaka Castle. Kusunoki's troops had built a two-layered protective wall around the castle. Kusunoki's warriors cut the ropes between the layers when invaders tried climbing the wall. The first layer fell away, taking the climbers with it.

Samurai were expected to be both clever and daring.

Samurai might serve a lord, a shogun, or the emperor. No matter whom they served, samurai were expected to be unfailingly loyal.

When these techniques failed, Kusunoki came up with a new plan. Kusunoki ordered troops inside the castle to drag the bodies of fallen soldiers into a pile. Then they set the pile on fire. As the flames rose, the fire distracted the shogun's forces. Kusunoki and his men escaped. The shogun's soldiers eventually entered the burning castle. They found the burned bodies inside. They assumed their enemies had committed suicide to avoid surrendering. Kusunoki and his men had faked their own deaths.

Even though they had been trying to kill him, the shogun's men praised Kusunoki's courage. But the great warrior was a well-trained samurai. He used cunning plans to overwhelm the enemy and convince them to retreat.

FURTHER EVIDENCE

Chapter One introduced famous samurai warrior Kusunoki Masashige. Read back over the chapter. What do you think the text is telling you about who this man was and what he valued in life? Go to the Web site below to read more about Kusunoki. Find one or two quotes on the Web site to support the chapter's main ideas about him. Do the quotes reinforce what you've already learned. Or do they tell you something new about him?

Kusunoki Masashige
www.britannica.com/EBchecked/topic/325541/Kusunoki-Masashige

THOSE WHO SERVE

Extreme loyalty was not the only important qualification for being a samurai. A samurai also needed extensive training in the martial arts. He needed good-quality weapons, sturdy armor, and a horse. Most importantly he needed wealth in order to be able to afford these things.

Becoming a samurai warrior meant getting the right training and the right equipment.

The Rise of the Samurai Class

The Taiho code of 702 established a Japanese army consisting mostly of foot soldiers. The soldiers were from the peasant class. The peasant soldiers did not have a choice about serving in the military. The royal court forced these men into service.

These farmers-turned-soldiers had spent most of their time working in the rice fields. They had not studied archery or sword fighting. They did not always have the martial arts skills necessary to compete against well-trained invaders from foreign lands.

The style of warfare began changing. Soldiers on horseback became more useful than soldiers on foot. Horses were expensive. It took a lot of money to buy grain to keep horses fed. Rich nobles lived on large estates that had enough land to keep horses. Peasants usually farmed small plots of land owned by the government. These peasants had little to no space for a horse.

Warriors from wealthy families gained an advantage when Japanese soldiers began riding horseback.

Noblemen trained in the martial arts began replacing the peasant-class military. These new warriors often came from families living in the eastern provinces beyond Kyoto. In exchange for their service, these warriors received more land from the emperor. Having more land meant having more power. These warriors soon became known as the samurai.

Family Ties

A samurai's lineage was extremely important. Whenever possible a warrior would sit on his horse shouting out the names and heroic deeds of his ancestors before engaging in combat. However, this could be very difficult in the heat of battle. Another way for a samurai to announce his lineage on the battlefield was to carry a banner with his family history written on it.

A Ruler in Name Only

This era of Japan's history was known as the Heian period. It was an era of peace. This period of very little warfare lasted from 794 to 1185. At this time, Kyoto was an elegant and comfortable place. Members of the imperial court passed much of their time doing relaxing and fun activities. They composed poetry and watched sumo-wrestling matches. They attended festivals and played games such as backgammon.

The wealthy and powerful leaders in the city were busy having fun. At the same time, rural samurai families competed with one another for control of the countryside. The imperial court had given these

Because the Japanese court was not focused on ruling, samurai went to battle to settle disputes among themselves.

land-holding nobles authority to govern the rural provinces. Samurai collected taxes and enforced the laws. As a result, the emperor began to rule in name only. The samurai gained more power. Soon certain clans began dominating other samurai families. These dominant clans usually had the most land. The entire warrior class grew in power.

This screen shows the battle between the Taira and Minamoto clans, two powerful Samurai families.

Shogun for Life

Two samurai families emerged as the mightiest in the land toward the end of the Heian period. The Taira and the Minamoto families often fought against each other. They also fought among themselves. Certain members of the Taira and Minamoto clans supported one heir to the imperial throne. Other members supported another heir. Things came to a head in 1156 with a short civil war in the streets of Kyoto. The conflict was known as the Hogen Disturbance. The fighting lasted only one night. But it was a sign of things to come.

Female Samurai

A woman's role in a samurai family was to tend to household tasks and take care of the children. Samurai men were often away at war or looking after their estates. Many women needed martial arts training to protect their homes from intruders. The *naginata* was an especially popular weapon for women. A naginata was a long pole with a blade at the end. It allowed a woman to fight effectively. However, it kept a distance between her and her attackers.

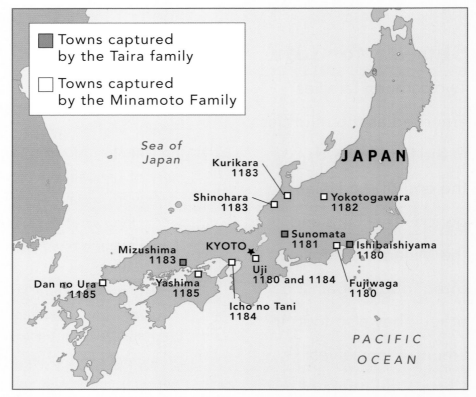

The Gempei War 1180–1185
From 1180 to 1185, members of each of the Taira and Minamoto families battled for control of Japan. They took over different cities across the country. This map shows Japan at the time of the Gempei War. It also shows the years each family gained control of Japanese cities. How does this map help you understand the information on the Gempei War in this chapter? What new information does it provide?

The Hogen Disturbance set off a chain of events that led to the Gempei War. The Gempei War was a struggle for dominance between the Taira and Minamoto clans. First one family came out on top,

EXPLORE ONLINE

Chapter Two focused on the history of samurai warriors. It talked about who the samurai were and how they came into power in Japan. As you know, every source is different. The Web site below also discusses samurai warriors and their history. How is the information in the Web site below different from this chapter? How is it the same? Did you learn anything new from the Web site?

Samurai

www.pbs.org/empires/japan/enteredo_8.html

then the other. Finally, in 1185, a fierce samurai named Minamoto Yoritomo led his family to victory.

Minamoto set up a stronghold outside of Kyoto, in the plains of Kamakura. He declared himself shogun for life. Until then, shogun had always been a temporary position. Minamoto was changing the rules to give himself more power.

Minamoto was still in the service of the emperor. But he set up his own shogunate, or military government. Because of this, he achieved much more authority than had past shoguns.

The age of samurai rule had begun.

CHAPTER THREE

THE WAY OF THE WARRIOR

Samurai Takezaki Suenaga rode into the city of Kamakura, Japan, in August 1275. He was prepared to finally receive the recognition he deserved. Takezaki had proven himself in battle against the forces of Kublai Khan in 1274. Kublai was a Mongol emperor from China. He had hoped to claim Japan as part of his empire. The troops of the shogun met the invaders as their ships landed on the

Typhoon winds helped Takezaki Suenaga and the other samurai beat the Mongols. The winds seriously damaged the Mongol ships.

Japanese island of Kyushu. Takezaki threw himself into the thick of the action.

After much fighting, the Japanese were able to hold off the invaders. Takezaki expected to receive the usual rewards from the shogun as thanks for his role in the victory. He expected a gift of land. He thought he might get a horse or two. The shogun's praise would also be a highly valued reward.

The Samurai Code

A samurai acted entirely in the service of his daimyo, or lord. The daimyo might be the emperor, the shogun, or a fellow samurai in a higher social class. No samurai could serve two masters. A samurai was loyal to his master until death. Sometimes this loyalty lasted generations. A samurai's family served his lord's family long after that samurai had died.

Bushido

Takezaki demonstrated many of the qualities of the samurai code in the fight against the Mongol invaders. Loyalty, dignity, bravery, discipline, acceptance of pain, and death were all part of the

Takezaki made sure his name would live on by having a series of full-color scrolls painted to show his accomplishments.

samurai code of behavior. As centuries passed, this code came to be known as *bushido*, or "the way of the warrior."

When the battle ended, however, Takezaki's commanding officer failed to report his honorable fighting to the shogun. Takezaki had no proof that he had performed as fearlessly as he said he did.

Takezaki spent two months in Kamakura. Finally, he was granted permission to speak to the chief in charge of giving rewards. Takezaki said that the chief should cut off his head if Takezaki's account of his actions in battle proved at all untrue. The chief believed him. Takezaki kept his head. He also received an estate on the island of Kyushu and a new horse. He helped the shogun defeat the Mongols again when they attempted another invasion in 1281.

Samurai Weapons and Armor

Samurai in earlier times had primarily fought with arrows shot from long bows. These bows were made out of wood and bamboo. By Takezaki's day, the types of weapons had expanded to include many handheld swords and daggers.

A samurai charged at the enemy with his *katana*. This was a long, curved sword used for fighting on horseback. Takezaki and his fellow warriors used katanas to knock rivals off their horses. Once an opponent was on the ground, the samurai drew a *tanto*, a type of dagger. Then he would deliver a deadly blow. Finally he cut off the dead man's head.

Samurai Weapons and Armor

This image shows samurai weapons and armor in the 1000s. Based on the information presented in the text, how might a samurai have used each of these weapons in battle? Take a closer look at the samurai's armor. What specific parts of the armor might help protect the samurai? Use information from the text to back up your answer.

Takezaki protected his body from attack with the traditional style of samurai armor. This armor was constructed from small rectangular plates, called lamellae. The lamellae were made from iron or rawhide. The lamellae lay in overlapping rows connected by leather or silk cords. They looked a bit like shingles on a roof. The lamellae absorbed

Off With Their Heads

Custom allowed a samurai to cut off the head of each opponent he killed. He could bring those heads back from the battlefield for his daimyo as trophies. This practice was so common that samurai going off to war tied their hair into fashionable topknots. They also groomed their faces before entering combat. They wanted to look dignified even if they ended up losing their heads. As a show of respect, the victors often cleaned their opponents' heads before presenting them to a daimyo.

shock very well. This type of armor could not be pierced easily. The lamellae were covered in a lacquer. This made the armor shiny and protected it from weather.

With sturdy armor and deadly weapons, samurai were dangerous warriors.

The Hagakure, meaning "Hidden Behind the Leaves," was a guide to samurai beliefs and practice. Yamamoto Jocho wrote the guide in the 1700s. The book describes the concept of bushido:

> *Bushido, I have found out, lies in dying. When confronted with two alternatives, life and death, one is to choose death without hesitation. There is nothing particularly difficult; one has only to be resolved and push forward. . . . Conversely, as long as one's choice is death, even if he died without accomplishing his just aim, his death is free of disgrace, although others may term it as a vain or insane one. This is the essence of bushido. If one, through being prepared for death every morning and evening, expects death any moment, bushido will become his own, whereby he shall be able to serve the lord all his life through and through with not a blunder.*
>
> Yamamoto Jocho. The Hagakure—A Code to the Way of the Samurai.
> Trans. Takao Mukoh. Tokyo: Hokuseido Press, 1980. Print. 35.

Back It Up

In this passage, Yamamoto Jocho is using evidence to support a point. Write down a few sentences describing the main idea of Yamamoto's passage. Then write down two or three pieces of evidence that support this main point. How does this evidence support Yamamoto's main idea?

CHAPTER FOUR

FROM WAR TO PEACE

War meant work for the samurai. It meant they were needed. Their services proved especially valuable during the *sengoku jidai,* or the "age of the country at war." This era was also known as the Warring States period. This period of intense conflict lasted for more than 100 years. It began in 1467 and lasted until 1568.

Finding work to do was not a problem for most of the samurai's history.

Individual leaders across Japan began seeking more power. This meant constant fighting among the Japanese lords and clan leaders. The emperor had little control over his citizens. Even the mighty shogun failed to restore order. Samurai aligned themselves with a clan leader or daimyo. The battles led to big changes in the social order. Formerly noble clans lost everything. They disappeared from the social and political scene. But some lower-class families' fortunes rose with their military victories.

One samurai who climbed to the top of the heap was Toyotomi Hideyoshi. He worked hard to unite Japan through peaceful and military techniques. He could not be a shogun because he did not come from an elite family. Instead he became the head of a group of daimyos in the now united country in 1585. The sengoku jidai was over at last.

Out of a Job

In the 1600s, Japan began a few hundred years of relative peace. The Tokugawa samurai family took

Toyotomi Hideyoshi helped bring peace to Japan. But the new era of peace meant troubles for samurai warriors.

over the shogunate. One of its first orders of business was to close off Japan to foreign trade. The country remained isolated from the rest of the world until the 1800s.

Life was very different for samurai under the Tokugawa family rule.

Samurai life was very different during times of peace. Instead of preparing for battle, samurai wrote poetry. They performed tea ceremonies. They participated in and watched a popular form of Japanese theater called *Noh*.

Many samurai looked for a new line of work. Some took positions in the Japanese government. Others trained to become Buddhist priests. Some samurai opened martial arts schools.

Masterless Samurai

With no wars to fight, daimyos no longer needed to acquire samurai. A samurai with no master to serve was called a *ronin*. Ronin sometimes turned to crime to make a living.

A popular legend in Japan concerns 47 ronin. Lord Asano had been the ronins' master. He was ordered to

Firepower

Japanese weapons changed as technology improved. In 1543 Portuguese traders brought an early style of gun into Japan. Japanese craftsmen eagerly examined this new weapon. They soon began manufacturing guns. Firearms were easy to move, effective, and easy to keep up. Some samurai used firearms. But most saw it as dishonorable. These early guns were less precise than modern weapons are. It took many soldiers to use the guns effectively against an enemy army. A samurai with a bow and arrow and good aim could work alone.

The 47 ronin were said to have killed a shogun official who caused their master to commit seppuku.

commit seppuku after attacking one of the shogun's top officials inside the shogun's palace. After Lord Asano's death, his samurai decided to take revenge. They left their lord's castle. Then they wandered the countryside separately for one year. They wanted the official to believe he was safe. After a year apart, they met up to attack the official's estate. They killed the shogun's official and many of his samurai.

Men of Legend

In 1868, Emperor Meiji restored the imperial court to a position of supreme rule over the country. The reign of the shoguns ended for good. Japan adopted a modern, Western-style military. The samurai passed into the realm of myth and legend.

Samurai still live on in cultures around the world. Samurai warriors have been the subject of countless books, paintings, statues, movies, and comics. The stories of their bravery and their accomplishments in battle grow more epic with each retelling. People still study samurai skills, such

The Last Samurai

Saigo Takamori is considered to be the last true samurai. Saigo was born in 1828. He was loyal to the emperor and hated the Tokugawa shogunate. He fought tirelessly to restore power to the imperial court. Eventually Saigo grew bitter. He thought the new government treated the shrinking samurai class disrespectfully. He helped stage the unsuccessful Satsuma Rebellion against the emperor in 1877. He was either killed in the fighting or committed seppuku.

There are no modern samurai warriors. But people can still train in the art of samurai sword fighting.

as swordplay. Samurai also live on in the Japanese people, who value loyalty and honor. They take pride in their ancestry in the same way their ancestors, the samurai, did.

Martial arts master Miyamoto Musashi wrote *The Book of Five Rings* in 1643. In the following passage, he describes the best mindset to have when facing an opponent:

> *As I see the world, if a burglar holes up in a house, he is considered a powerful opponent. From his point of view, however, the whole world is against him; he is holed up in a helpless situation. The one who is holed up is a pheasant; the one who goes in there to fight it out is a hawk. This calls for careful reflection.*
>
> *In large-scale military science as well, opponents are thought of as powerful and dealt with carefully. When you have good troops, know the principles of martial arts well, and sense the way to overcome an opponent, you need not worry.*
>
> Source: Miyamoto Musashi. The Book of Five Rings. *Trans. Thomas Cleary. Boston: Shambhala Press, 2005. Print. 58–59.*

Consider Your Audience

Read the passage closely. How would you adapt it for a different audience, such as your parents, a younger sibling, or your friends? Write a blog post that conveys this same information in a way that can be understood by the new audience. How is your blog post different from the original text?

IMPORTANT DATES AND BATTLES

702
The Taiho codes call for a peasant-class military in Japan.

794
The Heian period begins. Authority begins shifting from the emperor to rural clan leaders.

1180
The Gempei War begins between the Taira and Minamoto families.

1336
Kusunoki and his troops fight for Emperor Go-Daigo's restoration to the throne in the Battle of Minato River.

1467
The *sengoku jidai*, or the "age of the country at war," begins. Samurai reaches their height of influence during this time.

1543
Portuguese traders bring the first guns into Japan.

1185

Minamoto Yoritomo and his family win the Gempei War, taking control of Japan.

1274

Kublai Khan's fleets invade Japan, but samurai warriors fight them off.

1331

Legendary samurai Kusunoki Masashige and his men use a variety of clever tactics to fend off attack from the shogun's men during the siege of Akasaka Castle.

1585

Samurai Toyotomi Hideyoshi becomes the leader of a united Japan.

1868

Emperor Meiji dismantles the Tokugawa shogunate and makes himself Japan's supreme ruler.

1877

Saigo Takamori, the last samurai, dies after a failed rebellion.

Dig Deeper

What questions do you still have about the samurai? Do you want to learn more about their armor? Or their weapons? Write down one or two questions that can guide you in doing research. With an adult's help, find a few reliable new sources about the samurai that can help answer your questions. Write a few sentences about how you did your research and what you learned from it.

Why Do I Care?

The last samurai warrior lived hundreds of years ago, but your life might not be so different from the samurai. Have you ever fought hard for something you believed in? Does your family follow any special traditions? Write down two or three ways the samurai and their way of life connect to your own life.

Tell the Tale

This book discusses how important it was for a samurai warrior to remain loyal to his lord. Write 200 words that tell the true story of a young samurai warrior pledging loyalty to a lord. Be sure to set the scene, develop a sequence of events, and write a conclusion.

You Are There

Imagine that you are Kusunoki Masashige's son. How does it feel to watch your father go into battle? What is your life like? What expectations does your family have for you? How is your life different than it would be today?

GLOSSARY

armor
a covering that protects someone's body during battle

clan
samurai family

daimyo
land-owning lord who samurai served

heir
person with a legal claim to a throne when the current ruler dies

imperial
relating to the emperor

lacquer
clear varnish painted on samurai armor to give it strength and shine

lineage
a person's ancestry

martial arts
arts of combat or self-defense

ronin
samurai who don't serve a master

shogun
supreme military leader of Japan whose office existed from AD 1192 to AD 1868

shogunate
military government led by a shogun

siege
the act of surrounding and attacking a well-defended place

LEARN MORE

Books

Dean, Arlan. *Samurai: Warlords of Japan.* New York: Children's Press, 2005.

Duey, Kathleen. *Samurai.* Edina, MN: ABDO, 2006.

Macdonald, Fiona. *How to Be a Samurai Warrior.* Illustrated by John James. Washington DC: National Geographic, 2005.

Web Links

To learn more about samurai warriors, visit ABDO Publishing Company online at **www.abdopublishing.com.** Web sites about samurai warriors are featured on our Book Links page. These links are routinely monitored and updated to provide the most current information available.

Visit **www.mycorelibrary.com** for free additional tools for teachers and students.

INDEX

ABOUT THE AUTHOR

Christine Heppermann is a columnist and reviewer for *The Horn Book Magazine*. She has also published poetry in literary journals for adults. She has an MA in children's literature from Simmons College and an MFA in writing for children and young adults from Hamline University.